Between a Rock and a Herdwick

1. Between a Rock and a Herdwick
2. TuT
3. Mannanin's tree
4. Dance to a distant drum
5. Mothers Ruin
6. The Scarecrow festival
7. The Fishers Bride
8. Silent Whispers
9. When does it end?
10. Diary of a drinking man
11. Easter!!
12. Home again (The visit)
13. In no particular disorder
14. Pictures
15. Blackpool
16. The Tower Ballroom
17. Having one's cake
18. The beginnings
19. Well!
20. Static!
21. Gland nut
22. The Manx Way
23. Ain't no stopping me now
24. Legends from forgotten days
25. 'twas only love
26. Stripped clean
27. Being four
28. Shattered portraits
29. The free pen or (Has anyone seen my prostate)
30. Songs of summer
31. Eastfield
32. Stay calm
33. The early years
34. Adrift
35. Aliens
36. Haworth
37. I just don't!
38. Result!
39. Extracts from the second book of qunts (The Hunt)
40. Remembrance
41. Beach
42. Silent Love

43. Who's on the table now?
44. Tomorrow
45. Round here!
46. Andy & Freddie (on the cart that we repaired)
47. The wrong inflammation
48. Hopping & bopping
49. When does it end
50. The pandemic express
51. There will always be somewhere
52. Well trained
53. Within my grip
54. Tough Times
55. The blue nylon rope
56. Where do you see yourself...
57. Fields of screams
58. Operation orchiectomy
59. Where the hearth knows no stranger
60. Sands of time
61. Easing in
62. Still here
63. Sometimes it isn't me
64. ABC
65. Things I miss most
66. Ode to Illiam
67. Thanks to the memories
68. On the sunny side

Between a Rock and a Herdwick

These days!
My eyes struggle the well worn paths of others
reaching ever higher
higher than I would see my own feet clamber
blinking and stumbling beyond their ability to focus
I slip past these bold strangers as they cling to each new view
searching souls between rock, crag and Herdwick

Old eyes
flicker through thoughts of ancient hills
climbed as a boy
recalling the pains and joys of slipping
tripping the grassy paths of youth
memories fall like un-tendered stone walls
details lost and buried in the scree of time
an empty lime kiln reminds me of my fate
thoughts cold and old as the slate grey posts
with neither gate nor tie
they drift as ghosts
both pasts and present pass me by

The hard grey slate of the Isle of man
softens as I recall how warm it felt
baked in summer sun
how it glistened
how it pillowed my head as I listened to skylarks
or watched in wonder
lost in the jet-streams high above

How soft it felt
beneath my feet in rivers flow
how cool it touched
when ere we dipped a toe
names of lovers
gently scratched within a heart
dumb struck through with arrows
some loves unlike lovers
never part.

I know what a hill looks like!
I see the beauty in these mountains
in dales and dells
in Cumberland and Reiver
in Westmorland and fells
to me! No more than strangers
cold and hard

(between a rock cont:)

foreign rocks on which to park this offcumdens bones
empty homes cling to forgotten pastures
only the Herdwick finds comfort on this edge
hedgers
no longer able to hold back the relentless trek of the invader
a new found boot on route to foul their own view

I'd like to climb just as I did
as a kid
as sure footed as a Herdwick
young and quick
not rutted in the past
To once more follow instinct and
cast aside old assumptions
that you're going the wrong way
way off the well worn path
a stray!
far away from its Shepherd
far from the fetch
far from the barking beast
that!
At very least
should be my goal

Well it was when I started
It was in my soul
Within my reach
and so!
I allow my eyes to climb
past the well worn paths of others
past slate strewn lines from lovers
past the lost walls and the scree
to the past
where once I clambered free.

Tut

I've just been shot by an aged assassin
a geriatric sniper
a rifle tongued sharp shooting wrinkly
"TUT" she muttered
and it hit me like a bullet
full on
stopping me cold
dead in my tracks
guttered
and without looking back
she was gone

it's impossible to recover from something like that
it buries itself deep
it repeats in acid indigestion
Tut after Tut after Tut
In time
it will fade
it will stutter its way
into that darkened corner of your mind
where mistakes are stored
and there it will sit like a lie
like a bored child
that is always asking you
why?
Bloody Tut!!!

Mannanin's tree

Beneath a mountain
in the shadow of a hill
beneath a tree
beside waters calm and still
I sat me down
in memories of the lost
throwing pebbles, watching ripples
and reflecting on the cost

Beside me sat a man
a man I'd never met
and yet it seemed! I knew him
Maybe my father knew him
I could tell he knew my family
I could tell he knew me well

And you are? he asked
and I questioned "but you know me!"
Yes he replied.
But who are you really?
Are you who you think you are?
or do you just think "you're you"!
in truth
I didn't know
I didn't know what the hell he was talking about

Not until he stood and turned to walk away
"Time enough" he said! "time enough for all"
and then I knew!
it was as if he'd ripped a pebble from a pond
and the ripples flowed inward
back to the center from somewhere far beyond

"I am everyone!" he said
I am all who went before me
I am all that's yet to be
I am the past
I am the present
I am they and they are we
I am my father, my mother, my brothers
I am my sisters
I hold the blistered fingers of my forefathers
as they have held my own

Beneath any mountain or any tree
in shadow or in sunlight
I am home and I am free
for I am as they were, as they were to me

Who am I?
in part I am that man I met
I am Manx
I am Mannannan MacLir
Well!
 I am beneath this tree!

Dance to a distant drum

I hear in my mind
the distant Bodhran
like the beat of a heart
in the heart of the man
a beat unmistakable
rhythmic and clear
ever so far
yet ever so near

I see in my mind
a boy seventeen
cool as a cucumber
and yes! Just as green
a boy on the brink
of becoming a man
and it's all in a blink
and it's all a man can

and I still smell the two stroke
that ran through our veins
out through our boots
and down through the drains
I remember the cold
through the heat of the thrill
brothers together
heading over the hill
We've drunk in the rain
had whiskey galore
had laughter for breakfast
and for dinner, some more
and the evenings we've spent
spending into the night
rendering wrongs
rendered everything right

(distant drum cont:)

and now in the distance
I hear the Bodhran
as it lays down the beat
as only one can
So set free the mind
let the fiddlers play
and in song and in laughter
we shall dance one more day
dance one more day shall we
dance one more day
let the music play on
let us dance one more day

Mothers Ruin

Mother's apron strings
are as barbed as bee stings
tied and tethered hooks
looks that blind
guilt always finds you
ties you down and binds you
permanent to the breast
mummy knows best
and you know if you pull away
it will kill her
they'll say!

It pays to be
mummy's little helper
mummy's little darling
mummy's little baggage
with a breast pump full of Carling
fifty plus and in retreat
pouting!
still hung out to dry
upon that teat

I suppose there is a certain reluctance
to except that!, or admit that!
there may be some underlying attachment issues
that may need to be addressed
although!
I must confess
I am somewhat detached
as mother licks another tissue and wipes my face

Don't get me wrong!
There is a place
for mothers and sons

(mothers ruin cont:)

it's on Sundays
it's that one day of the week
when they kiss your cheek
when the child comes a man and allowed to speak
and they seem so old and frail and weak

oh I love those days
those now so not so often days
those days when you and yours can come
those equal playing fields of fun
as childer scamper round our feet
now there's a joy
there is a treat

You can see it in their faces
pure joy
traces of you when you were......
you know?
like the ones you brung

I think
once all the leaving's done
once all the waves and kissed goodbyes have gone
that mothers
sit behind an ever open door and smile
resting in the silence from the din
and the presents of you there
still struin across the floor
and all the more them knowing
It was only mothers ruin
that dragged you in

The Scarecrow festival

Three little pigs
Diddle Diddle John
Hey diddle diddle
The sheep have all gone
Tom in the corner sucking his thumb
Little Jack Horner
Twiddle Dee
Twiddle Dumb

The wind did make the baby sway
Hickory Dickory ticking away
Goosey Goosey
Jack and Jill
Sponge Bob Square Pants
Ben and Bill

A crooked man
A crooked tanner
A crooked Cat
And Polly Anna
Humpty Dumpty
Little Boy Blue
Wee Willie Winkie
Winnie the pooh

(scarecrow festival cont:)

Pussy Cat Pussy Cat

Where have you been?

Chasing blind mice

But they never seen

Incie Wincie

Jumping about

Up and down that water spout

Noddy, Thomas

Fireman Sam

Mary with her little lamb

A scarecrow with a lollie pop

Causing all to stand and stop

Raining Pouring Snoring Man

Mary's quite contrary plan

Sing for sixpence

Pepper a pig

Ride a Cock Horse

Jiggerty Jig

The king just sat there all surprised

Miss Muffet never realized

Cock a Doodle, Doodle Doo

An old woman in a shoe

Spring and summer

Winter too

But My! how that boy's turned blue

The Boys and Girls came out to play

With Scarecrows on an autumns day

The Fisher's Bride

She hooked me with her eyes

And lit her lips a smile so warm

It set the sun

And there beneath a moon filled sky

A lonely heart was won

She cast her hair

and there in love's entanglement

I was lost and floundered there

Silent Whispers (to all the children caught up in man's conflicts)

No one's there to whisper them goodnight.
No one sings them nursery rhymes, or tells them it's all right
No one smiles a greeting, to aid them through the day
No one's there to see them grow, in confidence and play
No one calms their cries for help, no kisses for the cheek
Just, here's your world in a box, inheritance of meek
No care parcel, contains a mum or dad
There's not a package big enough, to replace the life they've had
Every little package, just reminds them of their plight
If only someone whispered them goodnight
Tell them that God loves them, tell them if you dare
Explain to them the mystery, as to why he's left them there
Wrap it in a package, drop it from a plane
Place your conscience in a box, if it helps you dull your pain
Place beside a little bowl of rice
Place your hand upon your heart, and tell them God is nice
Suffer little children, a message from on high
Wrap them up in gratefulness but don't expose the why
Don't expose the sniper with the parents in his sights
And that no one's there to whisper them good-nights.
Don't expose the reasons, advertise your care
Advocate the innocent, defend why you are there
So late, so long, after all is gone
Afterwards is easier to see what's going on
We're geared for resurrection
Never ready for protection
We just sit and wait with helping hand
Give promises of better times, and hope they understand
Give them food and educate them of their rights
Yet no one's there to whisper them good-nights.
If only we could help them to their feet
Hold them in our arms, above the blood upon street
Remove the fear reflected in their stare
Wipe away the salty tear, reflected in the glare
Wipe away the memory, return to them their prime
Exonerate dependency, absolve them of the crime
Depended on the circumstance of origin of birth
Saline drip the future, so each man's salt is worth
Tell them it was just a dream, tell them it's all right
Tell them that you love them, and then whisper them goodnight.

When does it end?

The dog died
the same day as the fridge

the day the kettle element blew the power
shorting the electrics out at 98% of an update
I'd been downloading for several hours

Error followed error
error followed me
dialing 0 eight o eight hundred
thinking it was free

Calls from this number are chargeable
"SHE" said
"SHE"
told me to press 2
I did
and so it seemed
I was now number two
in a queue
With hindsight!
I probably should have pressed delete

Fifteen choruses
of someone's unfinished symphony later
the same voice informed me
that I was now number three in the queue

I had been virtually overtaken
I never did complete that call
so I'm not sure how it ends
although we do now have a Cat

Diary of a drinking man

Friday;
This week! I've been spending most of my time
trying to train my imaginary dog to sit
and although he has grasped the fundamentals
he still keeps me awake all night
with his constant barking

Tomorrow I'll buy him an imaginary bone
that should keep him quiet

Saturday;
The imaginary bone seems to work!
Hoping to get a good seven hours sleep
Will carry on with the training tomorrow

Sunday;
Took the Dog to the park
and let him off the lead
He ran off and didn't come back for ages
As you can imagine! "I wasn't very happy"

Monday
No sleep again!
Up all night looking for the bone
Imaginary dog imagined he'd buried it
Can't find it anywhere
but at leased now he will sit.

Tuesday
Found the bone!
He was sitting on it
Managed to get a couple of hours sleep
Back to work today
Hopefully he'll be OK on his own

Wednesday;
Can't believe it!
He's eaten all the post!
Bills! "everything" Gone!
No damage to furniture though, so that's a blessing
Can't find the bone

(diary of a drinking man cont:)

Thursday
He's had the post again
and I'm pretty sure I'd imagined I had a Budgie last week
that's also gone
but then so has its cage

Friday
Not looking forward to this!
Taking him to the Vets today
This is a bad day to be an imaginary dog

Friday Evening
Not quite as bad as I'd thought!
but the look on his imaginary little face
all that training and the poor little bugger can't sit

Saturday
He's gone!
I must have left the door open or something
Got up in the night. No Dog!
Called the police.
Well you can imagine their response
Bloody describe it!! (Cheeky bugger)
"Use your imagination" says I
(Perhaps someone broke in and stole your "Imaginary Dog" says he)

"Now we're starting to get somewhere" says I

Sunday
Never slept a wink
Bloody Budgies come back
only now it's got a ruddy bell!

Easter!!

I 'd like a chocolate Jesus
on a chocolate Maltese cross
or a chocolate virgin mother
on a bed of candyfloss
a bunny in a bishops hat
a church with chocolate bell
or anything religious
would suit me just as well

but all I get is rabbits
chickens eggs and then
the chicken that was in it
or a little chocolate hen
I'm not a disbeliever
nor am I devout
but if Easter is for Jesus!
Why do we leave him out?

So I'll eat my pagan chicken
on its little pagan legs
I'll eat my pagan bunny
and my pagan chocolate eggs
I'll stand around the alter
eating chocolate pagan mice
but a Christian cross with Jesus on
would surly taste as nice

Home again

Well here I am
home again
and nothing seems familiar
this house though somewhat similar
houses eighty thousand strangers
not a single trace of past
nothing that would last
a host of hollow faces
in an empty silhouette

Did I forget
to close a gate
or lock a door
although in truth
throughout my youth
we'd never locked the latch before

Open!

That was the thing of it
everything was open
an open house with an open fire
open hearts with a warm desire
to please
these were days of open minds
open souls
open dreams and open goals

but now they're locked
locked and bolted from the inside
Either that!
or someone's locked you in
like naughty children
trust you up in your lies
twisted and knotted
in suspicious ties of guilt

Is this the land our fathers built
Is this the land we sang of
an Island so free and so fair
though I do recall a place like that
and once!
I used to live there!

In no particular disorder

Do you have

It will only take

Have you ever been

Can I ask

Can you give

Can a representative call

Can we offer you it all

Can we claim at you expense

Are you due recompense

Were you to blame

Your call is very important to us

Unfortunately for them I'm covered

I suffer from a vary rare condition

CDD

Civility Deficiency Disorder

So I ask them to leave

Discourteously

by telling them to **Fuck Off**

Pictures

I drew me a picture
of me Mum and me Dad
and I coloured it in
with the memories I had
 Red Rosie cheeks on smiling eggs
pencil arms and pencil legs
Mother slim and dark and tall
Father with no hair at all
Both beset with big blue eyes
on crayon'd grass
'neath pastel skies

and how the days
they seems to fade
from summers glow
to winters shade
back then it seems
we always played
in colour
and then pictures made

Blackpool

If you broke Blackpool in half
you'd find there writ,
"Neglect"
a tower erected in
the memory of the can't be arsed
passed painters, long since flaked
take cover beneath facades
therein lurks the beggar
with the Rollex and their lot
and nothing for the poor
both penny and punter
tarnished
both worn faceless by the slot

Old time! Dancing

It's a bit like watching the dead tread water
water that had somehow solidified
to parquet
Music wafts like acrid smoke
consuming all within
above the din
an aged lady in a strapless gown
hears her God clicking fingers
in time with the past.

The Tower Ballroom

The organ rose from the depths
like the bridge of some long lost sunken frigate
at its helm
a captain!
At his command
volleys of octaves
fire across the ample bowed
most of which
completely miss their target.

Aged ladies, glitter-balled
stand in perfect Zymmetry
gentlemen wait
patiently
to be joined in the coo

Almost falling in the car-park
had resulted in terminal bruise
Somewhere down the line "she thought"
I think I've just blanked Noah!
They left the floor to an applause of hips
and a barely standing ovation

the singer!
just about managing
to hold his own to mimed music
he pumps his artificial leg to a Samba beat
proceeds to conduct a waltz
through fanatic games of patience
played out to the rhythms
of one, two, four
dresses shimmer as toupees dawn
on the glitter-balled heads
of the overly tanned
and the overtly free

In Purgatory
they played the Rumba
God taps his foot
and shouts
Next!

beneath the professionally taught
foundations of dance shudder
inept beginnings of what could be
yet another the failed attempt
of crossing a perfectly level floor
resume
regardless of the speed of step or beat
three minuets are never enough
and so the music dies
and the dancers move silent
theatrical in retreat

Having one's cake

In our village
On Wednesdays
I like to watch them eat cake
they only eat cake on Wednesdays
in the village hall
women of a certain age
with the occasional man
hemmed in

I've been that occasional man
duteously invited
and so delighted
to watch them eat cake
and there amongst the buns and biscuits
etiquette sits
a strict unspoken pecking order
off which I am bottom

I've seen them purposefully
not pick the larger of the slices
before it's offered
to the guest!
Me!
the non cake eater

Biscuits!
Oh of course I'll eat their biscuits
I'll drink their coffee
I'll drink their tea
I'll eat their scones with jam on
or without
it doesn't bother me

But mainly!
It's questions they offer me
it's why I've been invited
they have a menu
full of half baked ideas
mostly about me
about my family
and the why and the where and the who

it's hard to answer questions
with your mouth full of biscuits
so they learn very little
I risk a self invitation for seconds
and so!
off they go to bake
to take me back
and I will let them, eat cake

The beginnings

In the beginning
there was Man
then came Woman
with a plan
to change this strange
Neanderthal
to really nothing much
at all

Well!

I feel so well!
I was only telling the Doctor last week
how well I felt
as he removed his finger from my arse

and he said
everything seems normal
as normal perhaps as
defecating in a pot
or having one's testicles handled
by a complete stranger

now I've turned sixty
the world is obsessed with my impending doom
leaflets arrives on an almost daily basis
reminding me
of my mortality
monthly funeral saving plans

these agents of death
insure they have the required funds
to bury, burn or otherwise dispose of
my money and my earthly remains
and why not?
They've had my dignity!

Static!

The first day wakes slow
and drib by weary drab
the great unwashed scum past
until they form in endless stream
of seamless strife
an unfinished misspelled tapestry tattoo of life

the taboos of smoking
no exercise and a poor diet
have not yet reached the inner sanctum
of the socially housed
and so they puff and huff
in chains
trains of misplaced carriages
derailed marriages
single tickets
with no intention of making a return

Children cast adrift as blossom on the wind
each securing their own hard rock
on which to stamp their roots
where even there
they somehow grow to fast

Holidays are what you reward yourselves with
they are the prize to wit we've worked and strived
a goal
a quest for rest and solace
a place to reflect
this for a week or two
will be a home
a poor cheap copy of a home
a transparent home
a see through home
a home without heating
hot water
privacy

but a home non the less
and so
a week in

We join the flow
a caravan of fellow campers
we've become a part of the great unwashed
no longer strangers
but neighbours
a chap in front
asks me for a light
God how I wish I still smoked
in-fact
Static!
I might

The gland nut

My whole life
has been condensed
into something the size
of a walnut
a massive
all encompassing
life changing
endocrine of a nut
secretory nut
gland of a nut
in a nutshell
a cancerous cunt of a nut

She!
The doctor.
removes her finger
removes her latex glove
removes my dreams
leans slightly forward
I lean to the side
awkwardly
and although she mentions
Walnuts
amongst other things
I hear very little

What I did hear was
Cancer!
Oh I heard that
Oh loud and clear
now it's all I hear
it drowns out all other words
all other sound
all others
although now!

I can hear the ground
opening
I hear my dreams
scream and scratch
like fingers down a chalkboard
desperately reaching at life
grasping at life
witlessly snatching
greedy at the wistfulness of life
even the window glass
distorts my reflection

I left
clasping useless nuts
holding onto the clarity
of uncertainty

The Manx Way

Miles on miles on powdered tubing
Total loss or posi-lubing
Stretching out, pre-arranged
Gleaming chrome on pre-stretched chains
Pre-igniting twos and fours
Stroking engines, stroke pre-war
Vintage men on vintage metal
Faces worn with endless fettle
Sharing knowledge spares and jokes
Fairing well on feathered spokes

History born from many races
Different times and different faces
The comfort of a feather-bed
Combine with speed of thoroughbred
Combinations of child adult
Compliment the main assault
As son does shine on fathers bike
On footrests followed, like for like

Waxen women, weather worn
Whether or not to that manor born
Do often smile with poise and linger
Pour from life with oily finger
She's happy with her life and man
Darling pass the oil can
As he, on bended knee
Proclaims his love
 of riding free

Then!
From open road through open mega
Of rich man's toy or pride of beggar

They equalise the dream of boys
Where no one stands above the noise
As suck and blow with spark ignite
To bring to life and sparkle bright
The deep sheen gloss of polished paint
Reflects an age that time's made faint

Though
Not dulled in anyway the pleasure
That proof of standing there does measure
To view the capture of a bygone era
I feel brings Mann
A little nearer

Ain't no stopping me now

The World won't stop
it wont stop spinning
and I cant get off
and I don't feel I'm winning
Am I just too tired or just too lazy
to bother with the others
now it's all gone hazy

When was the beginning
where will be the end
will I find it on the internet
or should I phone a friend
Somewhere must be different
Is it all in vain
what's the point in questioning
the answers all the same

The world won't stop
My head keeps spinning
Which came first
the batsman or the inning
Don't look up; it's far too high
everyone is chocking
on irradiated sky
what's on telly
Who's on who
nothing really matters
if it's just my point of view
nothing really matters
if you're only flicking through

It just won't stop
everyone is spinning
who are all the looser's
if everyone is winning
I can't keep from crying
as the bastards sit there grinning
Where do all those happy people
keep their fucking souls
If God is in his heaven scoring goals
It just won't stop!

A legend from forgotten days

I found him the other day
Dieing!
That hard man from school
He lay cowering behind sunken eyes
Beaten by drugs
eaten away by his own lies
Lies I confessed to knowing
We each reach out a hand
Firm grips returned
and there we shook away our indifferences
back through time to friendship days
reminisced, through a single gaze

He seemed to abbreviate his being
to the point of having none
and then as if, it all flashed back
he thanked me for stopping by
tightening his grip like an age-d vice
he winked!
Grinned
I'm ok! He convinced
and he gave that "sorted look"
I've got some fuckin stories for your book
Cheers mate" said I
Cheers man" said he
We turned as we parted
as old friends looking back
over lives we'd started
Together
Stories" I thought!
If only he knew!
That man's a fuckin legend
of which there are few

Twas only love

Memories that shone
In the back of my mind
Fade into nothingness
Turning me blind
Happiness once
Was all I could find
Turn now my days into night

From the day we first met
The smile on your face
The times we have kissed
Through loves sweet embrace
To search for it all
Yet to find not a trace
Turns now my days into night

Love was a fever
That sweated my brow
Easier kept
Than regretting it now
I cannot recall
The why nor the how
Turns now my days into night

The heart that was beating
Beat the retreat
Broken and empty
To lay at your feet
Salts to the wound
Only bitter the sweet
Turns now my days into night

You were the first
Discarded in haste
The rest count for nothing
Just filling in space
The love that was lost
Is now laid to waste
Turning my days into night

Stripped Clean

I stand
on strips of green
between yesterdays
waiting on tomorrows plough
to turn me over

to grasp the four leaved clover
soiling the virgin
purging the land
killing my roots

new wave farmers
armed with writ and deed
plant their biannual greed
weeding out the poor

Moored hens contemplate
the dryness of their fate
nodding
as the rich probe boundaries
beyond their borders
and order their hardcore by email

they fail to grasp the consequence
of completely removing the fence
I shall knock my boots off
on lands now levelled clean
as the lounges lay there rotting
in tomorrows stripped of green

Being four

I can see your belly tum
are you the tubby telly mum
are you Dipsy thing or Poe
if not where did mummy go

Did you eat her
was she yummy
is that who's inside your tummy
did she squeal
did she shout
please please let my mummy out

Sometime later
all revealed
Daddy shouted
Mummy squealed
Mummy's tummy went away
A baby girl
has come to stay

A Shattered Portrait

Shattered!
I drift backwards through time
eyes stripped of colour
visions blurred
crawling through the absurd dreams of man
towards that blinding light
naked
twisted shards of futures lost
tear and shred my soul
useless follows useless
open goals lay un-scored
the poet stands ignored
and those who would be teaches
say I'm not to blame
I'm bored

Inside my head!
Where colour drips away
stripping the canvas to a blank day
I sit with silent pen to write
the harder things
that the harder man can't say

shall I write in colours
of a grey and fruitless past
those same old indiscretions
indiscriminately cast
the right account
the wrong accountant for the day
the right amount
and a mountain yet to pay

It's the right music
for the wrong song
and so rhythm counts for nothing
if the words come out all wrong
in the wrong shade
so here I'm am
just adding colour to memories I have made

The free pen or (Has anyone seen my prostate?)

Tomorrow!
I'm going to shit into a pot
Not a lot!
Just a little sample poo-pot
with a screw-top lid
slid surreptitiously
into a plain brown wrapper
a flat-packed crapper
popped into my local post box
there to be scooped up
by one of her majesty's representatives.

For a moment!
I ponder the sensitivity of a postal workers nose
as to whether or not they'll need to read the address

My life's a mess
I seem to be at that critical age
where everyone wants a piece of me
to cut and slice and dice and splice
my loins are numb and cold as ice
the cost may not be worth the price
and so the quest continues
to find that cancerous cell
and yet!
I feel so well, so full of life
so full of shite' as well one might

I was only telling the doctor the other day, how well I felt
as he removed his middle digit from my arse
and said "it feels normal!"
normal perhaps as shitting in a pot and posting it
or having ones testicles inspected by the state nurse
or worse
someone you know

Now that I've reached sixty
it seems the world and its aunty
are obsessed with my impending doom
as more shit hits the room
forcibly inserted through that "scat flap"
half opened it falls to the floor
more reminders of my mortality
Funeral saving plans
Begging letters from the agent's of death
ensuring they've insured my last and final breath
procuring the required funds for my disposal
what little there is left of me.

"Now then"
Where did I put that free pen!
To whom it may concern.
Has anyone seen my prostate?

Songs of summer

Sing me songs of summer days
when all my cares are flown
and there upon a vision raise
so I am ne'er alone
though my memories may lay silent
may they murmur near the shore
far across the emerald waters
to my homeland there once more

Sing me songs of storms and summers
sing me songs of hills and glen
sing me songs of wheels and water
sing me songs of fish and men
though the memories may lay silent
they may murmur near the shore
far across those emerald waters
like those fishermen of yore

Sing me songs of Ellan Vannin
tell me tales of Betsey Lee
take me back to calmer waters
where the air is sweet and free
lay my memories there in silence
let them murmur near the shore
lay my bones where e'er you find them
for my heart's at home once more

Eastfield

There's a field in my mind
from my youth where we played
where we fought and made friends
where we drank lemonade
where we climbed and we danced
through circles of straw
where we learned to ride bicycles
bogies and more
where mother would call out
to gather us in
and feed half the neighborhood
'long with its kin
and feeding on fruits
straight from the tree
my brothers my sisters
my family and me

There's a river that flows
through the back of my mind
where we splashed or we clashed
over treasures we'd find
where water flowed gently
o'er rapids or falls
where I still hear the laughter
my memory recalls
where skimming a stone
was a skill that was set
where we drank from the flow
without getting wet
where the poacher was king
of all he could steal
and the miller just borrowed
for turning his wheel

There's a hill in my mind,
where we used to slide
on sheets or on plastic
just for the ride
just for the hell of it,
just for the craic
for the straight coming down
or the strain climbing back
where Ravens would circle
the skies high above
where we've scattered the memories
of those that we love
where the views from the top
are the views I love still
My field my river
my memories my hill.

Stay calm

You can't hear me!
But in my head
I am screaming
screaming of something
or someone's name
wishing it, or them in vane
dead or worse
"In verse!"

A long loud stream of insanities
four lettered insults
inflamed profanities
stream my brain

Outside!
I am composed
properly postured
perfectly in control
I pose the consummate example of calm!

"He always seemed!" they'll say!
"A Very quiet!"
"Kept himself!"
"Wouldn't harm!"
Kind, Off Mann

But there! Upon a dusty shelf
amongst the poets, sits himself!
Proofed within the litter-arty
Jokes and joke books
the arty fart y
How to smile at any party
a self help book (How to stay calm!)
(without killing)

If at any point you find me smiling
Please don't ask

I may just be thinking of you!

The early years

My earliest memories of Clive, are of him returning home from having an operation to have a
kidney or something removed, and then of us riding to school on top of mothers big coach bodied
pram, which seemed to be huge, and indeed probably was considering the number of children she
had to transport. There were always babies in the house or should I say "the pram".
As children! We both had bears, Teddy bears! Cut from the same cloth, made the same from the
same hand and pattern, yet each, just like their keepers, would turn out to be very different bears
altogether.
My bear (John Teddy) was and adventurous bear, restless, always on the move, here there and
everywhere, pulled this way and that; shall we just say "played with"
Clive,s bear (James) on the other hand, was more of a "look how good I look sort of bear" a very
clean, very well groomed, "Very" man about town sort of a bear, wise beyond a bears years shall we
say, a bit like an older brother kind of bear; these bears would grow and play together, one a bit
rough around the edges and the other, well groomed and showing very little wear considering the
mileage, and together they covered some miles.
Some of those miles were covered on a 250cc Ossa Trials outfit, some of them even successfully,
but very few, We seemed to spend most of our time either stuck in mud, or sat on our backsides in it
wondering what happened, although when I say sat in the mud! It was mostly me in the mud and
Clive stood there looking very clean, though one day during a trial at Ellen Bane, I did manage to
submerge him completely, you're supposed to go over the Effin log not under it he exclaimed as I
unceremoniously dragged him to his feet.
Clive's most vivid memory of our trialing days. Is! As he was only too keen to recall.
when we set of together through a section, only for him to complete it on his own, "some feat" as it
was "he" who was supposed to be the passenger. Happy days though.
In fact! They've all been happy days, right from those first tentative steps, happy, happy days,
Well they were for John and James, and it is their story.

Adrift

I seem to-be adrift
mere flotsam on a sea of doubt
with time running out
a scuppered ship
a decommissioned rusting wreck
a bloated migrant on a foreign deck
up to my neck
in floaters

I'm out of my depth
communication fragmented
ammunition spent
Guns!
rusted with silence
with no aim, no rudder, no engine
with only one destination
I feel I've been torpedoed
by a rather large metallic dildo
and left to sink without trace

Eventually
I will slip beneath the waves
into the darkness
into the silence
into the grave
where the brave wait
where all who've gone before
have set their store

and there!
I shall have new guns
new munitions
new orders
a brand new rudder
fresh oil
and a bright new engine
I will set my compass to the stars
fix the horizon to my eye
to sail once more
farewell but not good bye

Aliens

Stand at the top of any escalator
in any shopping centre
any station
in any town
in every location
in any country
anywhere in the world
and tell me then
there are no aliens

at any junction
at any function
any juncture in life
there they are!
they cross our paths
they're in our field of view
they're in our fields
they're in our fuckin way
Aliens!

on bicycles
in cars
on planes
in between the fuckin stars
it's life on Mars
in pants in bras
they're in the drains
I hear them gurgling
as they chomp on Mackie Dee's
or scratch their brains
or show tattoos below their knees

The last elevator I was in
had three "No" four of them
smiling back at me
hiding in reflection in the polished steel
a full on family of shiny metallic aliens
just standing there
with not a care
they even got out on the same floor
the same door
those same aliens live with us now
to be honest
you'd hardly know we were there!

Haworth

A town
that history has steeped in servitude
enslavement to the Bronte brood.
Pilgrims to the page
wage war
against the well worn weathered heights of others
lovers tread foot-sore
stumbling
tripping tracks laid in fiction
short cutting whole paragraphs
just to be back before tea

It's not for me!
I'm not the type to tread the foul remnants of dog walks
though and in-between the pardoned pews
to stand in ore and stare
at pasts that once were never there

I shall instead
retrace the tracks within my mind
and there to find that curse
that is my own Kathleen
and love within that windswept verse
lost and cold and clean

I just don't!

I don't care if you think
I take to much sugar
or drink full fat milk
I wouldn't dare tell you
not to eat Tofu
how many rolls to take to the loo
I couldn't give a shit
If your clothes fit
in just that awkward way
that makes your arse look big

I don't care
how many times I've been told
or that the waters cold
or the last of what you wants been sold
I don't care if the duvet's old
or clothes are
incorrectly folded
the waters hot and scolded
your elbow

I don't care if you only wear jeans
only eat top branded beans
only bath and never shower
switch off plugs to save on power
save for holidays way past May
don't care what others think or say
liberal democrat or right
left or up or down with plight

I can't be arsed with fads or fuss
what's written on a big red bus
what's written in the paper stars
or eco warriors in eco cars
ego centered TV fame
the ones who point
to shift the blame
dancing dogs
barking mad
pregnant mum now pregnant dad
shots for shooters
cow-boys find
their saddled fillies
blinkered blind
Drunk

But for those of you who care for me
I'll give my all to all for free
for all who are and always there
the young the old and my own, my fare
my charge my loves my love my God
I want for no-ones odds or sod
Plus!
They really don't care what I think!

Result!

Tomorrow
I've got to shit in a pot
not a lot
just a little sample poo pot
with a screw top lid
slid into a plastic wrapper marked private
my own little plastic poo filled crapper
deposited at my convenience.

Seems science needs a part of me
it starts with blood then shite then pee
you must get tested
my life's become infested by parasites
intent on inflicting pain and paranoia

Do you suffer from any of the following?
Diarrhea
Incontinence
Constipation
Irritable bastard arsehole syndrome
but you might have cancer

"and you might not!"

and as the nation saves for its own funeral
the paranoid me
masturbates into a plastic paranoia pot
or maybe not!

Ah! Result!

Extracts from the second book of cunts

The hunt (new blood)
I've spent most of my life actively trying to avoid them
I mean you do!
You try to
although they're really hard to spot and so
a few slip though the safety zone
that invisible shield you wear
so you can call your own your own
and own your own
space

I'd always thought I'd met every kind there was,
so now was able to sniff out any trace
of them or their proximity
well that was until I met the leader of the hunt!
now there is a.......!

They enjoy it he implies
and so he leads his pack of lies
and blows a cowards tune
and tries to be both
immune and upfront
but now I see him his true colours
in bright bright red
blood red
and all I think is
Cunt!

Our cat's a ...... !
She scratches at our front door
and she knows full well
there is a cat-flap

Policemen
or woman I hear
both, man or on their manner do
from time to time must meet a few
one or two
they can tell you see,
but probably wouldn't tell me
I'm outside of their own community
without immunity or impunity
but the evidence is all there
once you've met one
you've probably met a pair

and the cat keeps scratching to be let in
and out and in and
the hunt goes on
for a fox that no longer exists in real time
these pissed up pardoned-heirs
way beyond their prime
prepare to mount

now both mount and mounted snort
set to hunt their fare
in a weak excuse for sport
no shortage of them there
abort abort abort

and the cat keeps scratching
in the hopes of getting in
like some frantic drowning swimmer
in an alcoholics skin
the door is locked
the boat has sailed
both bolt and boated gone
the master's in the doghouse
the hounds are on the run
the fox has flown
the cat has failed
the huntsman's blown his horn
the maid is on the registrar
and another cunt is born

Remembrance

a young man posed the question as the ranks march by the cenotaph ;
"look at that old cunt! I wonder what he did?"

Who's that old cunt with his hair all slicked
an' his legs all shot an' his hips all clicked
He's the last of the fallen of the old hand picked
is that old cunt! aye that old cunt!

Who's that old bitch with the shrapnel face
as she marchers past with amazing grace
she plugged the holes that the bullets traced
did that old bitch! yes that old bitch!

Who's that old Fokker with the carbide cough
shell shocked cocker with his balls blow'd off
he's got medals and the metal's rough
in that old Fokker and the Fokker's tough

Who's that sailor who was carried on the waves
a thousand strangers handshakes
saluting of the braves
He's the only son
but he's not the only dad
them the never knowing of the only sons they had

Out above the rankings stand the limp and stand the lame
sheltered from the trenchers where the blood and bullets rain
I'd call them politicians
but it adds to all our shame
excepting all the glory
yet will never take the blame

So who's the wanker in the pin stripped suit
sharp shooting banker with his hands on the loot
he supplied the bullets that the dying shoot
no subordination in the ranks
keep the compensation for the banks
keep the numbers coming
keep your eyes to front
if a man demands saluting
shoot the cunt

Beach

In the summers of our youth
we dipped our toes in the cool calm waters
ran with naked feet
built castles there
in sand and imagination
screaming at the waters in retreat

When autumn called
we've seen the fall
run hand in hand in love and play
built friendships there with one and all
and jumped and skipped the debris of the day

Winter with it's many moods
nips our fingers, chills our toes
it wraps itself around us
with an unforgiving grip
grabs us by the scruff
roughs us up
and discards us
sobbing and adrift

Spring brings in the new
new life
new dreams and aspirations
preparations for summer
and there too
to form new castles on old foundations
in defiance of the storms

Between the seasons
the sun bakes
the earth shakes
wind and flood do blow and beat
both man and daughter
in retreat

We are but flotsam
in its wake
on taken tides we ebb and flow
and so
to there we shall return
to once more calmly
dip a toe

Silent Love

I think!
I let a little part of me fall in love
I think!
a little part of everyone you ever met
fell in love with you

A little part of every man and every boy
a little part of every woman
shared the joy
each little girl, each child you taught
each gradu-ee
would fleet a thought
that you were theirs, and only true
belonged to them, and they to you

An indiscretion, so discreet
held by all and all so sweet
A silent love, within a heart
that only screams, now all's apart

and parting thus, we're part of you
we were the loves you never knew
we held you there in deep embrace
in far-flung loves, held face to face

and only now, should we regret
we didn't chance,when first we met
perhaps you knew, perhaps it's best
our silent love, be laid to rest

In memory of Marion Paige (a dear friend)

Who's on the table now?

In memory of mother's glass topped coffee table
Layered beneath the glass, a family tree of pictures

And there she'd sit, click,click, clickin'
baby clothes or knitty chicken
Mother Goose, I do despair!
I've seen Bob the Builder there!
and futures hatched and pasts recalled
glazed and polished overhauled
in easy reach of easy chair
the past and present gathered there
surrounded
framed by brood
memories born from motherhood

and in they'd walk one by one
two by two's and some by none
some by others, some by same
all for one but none in vain
Just passin'
just passin' through,
passin' time and memories too
stay a little, stop awhile
change a baby, exchange a smile
And who is that? And who's that mother?
and there she is oh that's the brother!
so many names, so many tiny faces
so many little buggers just to teach to tie their laces
teach to wash their faces, teach to....
look at little so and so, so cute there in her braces
as another grabs the apron strings, so used to changing places
There are traces of your father in you She said!
as I put my head in my hands
she told me! I had my grandfathers walk, and I wished I 'd had his hair,
Still !We're all there, all locked in time
those siblings, sons and brothers, all that ever passed that way, through sister, sire or lover
recorded in the best of days
cherished pictures by a mother.

Tomorrow

Tomorrow I'm turning over a new leaf
pack in smoking, drinking
I'm thinking of finding a new belief
one without Gods, Sod's law perhaps
follow that!
Everything that goes wrong
is meant to go wrong
being sods law
it may go right

Tomorrow
will see me in a new dawn
a new me
free from the shackles of mundane-eity
free to tackle Sundays without piety
without shopping
without popping into the pub
free from mind numbing sessions
with mates
no more dinners
welded to plates
staggered lunches
ducking punches
side plate certainties
on dead set hunches
with sides

Tomorrow no more Allad Jones
Turkey without bones
no more chuffin' Santa trains
with puffin' Santa clones
I'm cutting out the Christmas cheer
beer and mistletoe
though that my friend
would still depend
who's standing there below

But I shall change tomorrow
on this you have my word
there is no doubt
I'm coming out
this world is cursed and blurred
I'm stopping all the vices
what's passed as passed has passed
Why not today
I hear you ask
Well in truth!
I really can't be arsed

Round here!

Round here they talk of football
floods and foot and mouth
round here they talk of northern stuff
and stuff the fuckin south

Round here they talk
they talk of times
they talk of friend
from time to time
the time they spent
the rent

and everything they talk about
you know
they fuckin meant
to forget to mention
everything
and sod the fuckin tension

I met the neighbours
round here
they offer favours
some sugar
anther bugger
offered me
a pack of cheesy quavers
save them for the ravers
or until the next rounds yours

on Tuesdays they're closed
unless of course they're open
on a Monday
it's thinner than the water
is the beer they serve
on Sunday

round here
A she is he
and he is she
and we are they
and they are thee
should thee be wife or daughter
should we be tagged forever
by the things we've done
or ought'er

Round here
I know I'm no one
and you'd think
thee'd never care
round here
without you knowing
thee is almost no-one there

Andy & Freddie
On the cart that we repaired

It must have been the weekend
and it must have been quite dry
it could easily been a Saturday
or a Thursday in July
but was definitely morning
we were greeted by the soun'
of Andy hung on trailer
and Fred on tractor brown

"Have you got one of them water troughs?"
He enquired from off me dad
an' me father stood and nodded
and replied indeed he had!
"I'll take one if it's ready!"
said Freddie with a glance
"Can you stick it on yon trailer!"
and me father said "No chance!"

The trailer was a cobweb!
a frame upon two wheels
a five bar gate it wasn't
but it could have been it feels
"Leave it here" says father "
come back this afternoon
"I'll have Roger make a bed for it
and don't come back too soon!"

With the help of several scaffold planks
a dozen bolts or more
the trailer looked quite splendid
much better than before
we loaded up the water trough
my father Roge and me
When the boys returned that evening
father said the works for free

Oh they couldn't be more happy
and they thanked us times again
as they hitched up to the tractor
this brand new ridgid frame
and off they set together,
down the road and out of sight
waving out behind them
and bidding us good night

Now the next day started early
and it must have been the day
that followed after brothers
had took the trough away
when down the track comes Andy
and Freddie business bound
aboard their little white tractor
with a trailer they had found

it had bushes through the deckin
it had grass growd out the wheels
it had bits of string and plastic bags
where once there would be steels
there was cow muck, there was thistle
there was nettles by the score
there was nothing in the centre
where once there would be floor

"Can we have another water trough?"
 say Freddie "Mr Kneale!"
"No you ruddy can't! " says dad
and turns them on their heel
"I'll not be fixing all the scrap
that passes as a cart!
so you better drag yourselves and that
back home to where you start
you're welcome back tomorrow boys
as open mouthed they just stared
you can have another water trough
on the cart that we've repaired

Tomorrow came and went ya see
as tomorrows often do
and the water troughs still waiting
and us we're waiting too
we never seen them back again
and I doubt they paid the bill
I doubt they needed one more trough
and I doubt they ever will

The wrong inflammation

I don't know what you do with that!

You've got cancer!
That information
That inflammation that swells in your mind

Oh I think you'll find
"It'll be alright"
Must sound
a bit shite
a bit
Well!
it ain't you
It's marvelous what they can do!
to the few

and are you sure?
it's surprising what they get wrong nowadays

I heard of a poor woman
that went home with the wrong baby
so maybe
they got it all wrong
they got it, all fucked up

So hey!
maybe they'll take it away
cut it out
or zap it with radio waves
zing it and ping it and pang it it's gone
wing it and wang it and panic and pong
and so when do you see them again
Oh!
When will you see them again?

I looked him in the eye
and all I could see
was me!
Cowering there
unable to speak
Weak !

Why-s! Filled my head
along with the dying and the dead
and all I could think of was
Fuck!!!
Fuck Fuck Fuck Fuck Fuck

Hoppin' an' boppin' the blues away

In the corner of my mind
stands a youth in a drape suit
pointed shoes and hair a-quiff
stiff with brylcreem
Duck-tailed
Around his neck, a Bootlace tie
around his waist, a belt says "Don't"
no-one asks him why

and the music plays
and the Stray cat sways
and I'm lost within the beat
and the Ted's and Teens
and the in-betweens
all rock and rhythmic feet

Simmo, Ted and Trevor
Cooper, Zap, and Ron
Herbie bein' clever
Where did that cool cat gone?
Ginger, Fred, and Harry
Johnny and the band
and Angie who I married
how I loved to take her hand

Oh we've swung, we've swayed
we've danced, we've played
we've hopped in blue suede shoes
Now I'm standing on the corner
just boppin away the blues

When does it end?

The dog died
the same day as the fridge
the day the kettle element blew the power
shorting the electrics out at 98% of an update
I'd been downloading for several hours

Error followed error
error followed me
dialing 0 eight o eight hundred
thinking it was free

Calls from this number are chargeable
"SHE" said
"SHE"
told me to press 2
I did
and so it seemed
I was now number two
in a queue
With hindsight!
I probably should have pressed delete

Fifteen choruses
of someone's unfinished symphony later
the same voice informed me
that I was now number three in the queue

I had been virtually overtaken
I never did complete that call
so I'm not sure how it ends
although we do now have a Cat

The Pandemic Express

I heard it cough
Wheezing
Snottling
Chuffing and puffling
Whining and moaning
Griping and groaning
Splottering
Muttering and grotterling
Dithering and Dothering
Blithering and Blothering

They start
Do you have
It will only take a minute
Have you ever been
Can I ask
Can you give?
Can a representative?
Can we offer you?
Can we claim?
You are due!!!
Unfortunately for them
I'm covered
I suffer from a Civility Deficiency Disorder
So ask them to leave
Discourteously

Fuck Off!!

There will always be a somewhere

Somewhere in a parish
undiscovered
covered by years of fallen leaves
locked gates
shifted boundaries and blocked brakes
beneath a tree, beside a stream
where once a dreamer dreamt a dream
there, lies a wonder to be seen
for there had never ever been
a place so wonderful
so clean
so free
so full of me
and oh so perfectly Manx

Well Trained!

She stood there

Wagging the dog

"Good girl!" "Good girl!"

Thought the dog!

Within my grip

These are not the hands of a poet
these are rough worn callous hands
broken hands
with broken nails
black with hammer rash
sworn blue
scarred with stupidity

My father said:
the good lord only gave him
two little claws to scratch a living
I now know what he meant!

We scratch about
Chickens with bent backs
clinging to life's pecking order
ruffling our feathers
puffing out our chests
and crowing like the only cock on the yard.

By the end of a full day's scratching
my hands ache
my back aches
my brain's ached numb
with questions
When? Why? How?
and I only have three answers
nowadays
Yes
No
and 42
The latter!
curtesy of Douglas Adams

These are the hands
of a plumber
A builder
A joiner
A joiners mate
A father
A son

(within my grip cont:)

These hands!
Have held hands
held lovers
held the sleeping baby
comforted the crying child
nursed and soothed the tempered brow
Held life and death in equal grip
these hands still hold on now

With these hands
I can pick up a pen
thumb a page
press a key
or two or three
form whole words with just a touch
the press of a button
or the flick of a quill
from mind to finger tip
these old and life stained callous hands
form verse for minds to grip

Tough Times

It's a tough time to be a poet

It's not that I can't be bothered

nor I'm short of things to say

It's just I'm running out of alphabet

There seems less of it each day

Well!

Usable parts there off!

It's hard to start a sentence

Or say something off the cuff

Without offending someone

Or pissing something off

LGB, ITV + Q or I or BBC2 or

Plus or Bi

One has to ask the questions

Why?

But comment not!

Not I!

The blue nylon rope

Last week I bought a rope
A nylon one good and strong
Blue and long
I already had a rope!
Now I have two ropes!
Is that enough rope for a man?
I have no good use for either!

My hands are firmly tied by circumstance
and the knowledge insurance companies may question
the accidental fatality of my newly acquired
"tree climbing hobby"
For sale!
Two ropes
One as new
One careful owner

Where do you see yourself in five years?

Huddled in a doorway
on the threshold of despair
I for one quite clearly see myself
just sitting there
With!
Nothing in my pockets
nothing on my mind
hiding from a future
from a blind man lead by blind
and yet!
Even there
I'm in the way
under someone's feet
disrupting someone's day
littering the street
a discarded human
a broken flat pack of a man

all night seeing
cats hold their distance
even the rats ignore me
if only that were true of life
as the passing piss head pisses
drunken nobs and gobshites
kick my head

Tomorrow morning
I will wake to the warmth of my bed
and all of this!
will be a mental picture in my head
In the recurring beginnings of nightmares
This is where I see myself!
In five years!
In a home inside my head!
merely on the threshold
of being dead

I didn't get the job!

Fields of screams

In fields of dreams where children played
where fathers stooped and stooked the hay
where farmers reaped and sowed and ploughed became the oldon's we see now
the shoots they nurtured
way back then
tendered there to harvest men
should never ever end their day
in fields of blood and bullets spray

Operation orchiectomy(No cure for cancer)

Yes-today!
They squirreled away
Separating the squirrel from his nuts
No if's!
No buts!
No nuts!

Where the hearth knows no stranger

In the clear blue crystal waters
rise the green hills of my home
where the hearth it knows no stranger
and my heart is ne'r alone
the sky so grey above me
on the day I sailed away
shall be blue once more when I return
forever for a day

In those clear blue crystal waters
where when young we once did play
where the sea bird cries and laughter
mixed with children though the spray
and the sand so warm beneath us
and the sunshine in our eyes
through those long gone misted memories
I shall see your vision rise

in the clear blue crystal waters
I will sail to you once more
to the sound of Ellen Vannin
on the wind across your shore
In the clear blue crystal waters
rise the green hills of my home
where the hearth it knows no stranger
and my heart shall ne'r alone

Where the sands of time run out across the bay

When I leave
I'll leave my mind sitting on a beach
throwing stones into an ebbing sea
I'll be there with the sea bird
and in the child songs
drowning out the traffic noise
where boys dig holes
for reasons only they are aware
where sisters stare
through reflections in rock-pools
where factor 50
is only a small part of a mothers arsenal
as she digs deeper into her bag
for treats

I'll be
where memories gather at your feet
like shells upon a stony shore
in windswept sand and stormy spray
on summer eve
through winter's day
in setting sun
or breaking light
in calmed set sail
in seabirds flight

this is not the first time I've left my mind
to wander the beaches
or the inner
or outer reaches or some hill or dale
I often leave it there
for the days
recalled
a long forgotten shore
a tree
a view
but most of all
I leave it there
that I may share those memories
of you

Easing in

In the mornings
I like to feel the day on my skin
and let the daylight in
feel the weather
together
set ourselves
as one
me and the day
on our way to sunset

I bet
today is going to be
one of those days
one I may regret
or enjoy!
maybe one of those days
I recall as a boy
a joy filled day
a day to pass
day dreaming!

I'm not even thinking
of tomorrows
or even yesterday
but all the yesterdays
before!
before yesterday!
before the tomorrows
before the long forgotten days
the ones we've long forgot

I don't recall if we were hot!
or cold!
I remember being young
yet forget the growing old
When did that happen?
looking back on old days
forward to the new
up for inspiration
down on this and that and shoes

I don't have a list
of things to do
a shopping list of wishes
I'd be over half way through
in danger of just repeating myself
mundane after mundane
the same fucking thing
end of another
Ding!
end of another
Ding!
I like to feel the start of the day
against my skin
let it in
that's where I like to start
feel the weather
together
and ease the daylight in

still here!

If I just stood still
and never moved
just waited here
would life improve
would things around
remain the same
would I be blessed
or just be blamed

would things improve
or just be cursed
would sticking round
just make things worse
to shoulder blame
though not the fault
am I the wound
or just the salt
if I just stood still
and never move

Sometimes it isn't me

Sometimes!
It's hard to see where you fit in!
where you actually sit!
especially when life
conspires to fire curveballs at you
all you can do is duck

Sometimes!
just as you're getting used to
and settled into your human roll
the dice flips and what you thought of as a four
becomes a one
and no one really gives a

Sometimes!
the spots become spikes
likes! turn into angry words
catapulted back in furious rage
like angry birds spat venomously
from mouth to page

Sometimes!
thoughts of retirement turn to retreat
everything you thought you were
strewn about your feet
like scree!
there between the splintered shards
of memories
I see a man climb free

Sometimes!
I think!
"That" man
 isn't me!

ABC

Today
I'm in two minds
neither of which is particularly good
neither one is pre-thingamy
abcdef
fit for purpose
ie; thinking
I find myself caught up in an inner quandary
my memory not quite what it was
forgetting words like ! ....?
oh I don't know!
simple things.

Bells ring
and no one answers
memories of people without names
they have names!
I just don't recall them
Once upon a time
one mind would recall a memory
whilst the other
filled in the blanks
names etc, places
now it's just blanks
blank looks
and blanker faces

Is this my future
abc
or is this the future me
the forgetful me
stupid dim me
a man with a free mind
blind memories
a man with no past

I had a past
I had one last night
Yesterday!
Last month!
Last!
Years ago!
I had a past
Years ago I had a future
I don't remember it!
Being like this!

"Hello!!

"Not seen you in a while!"
"Who's this then?"

"Oh yes sorry! This is Nigel!"

"Hello Nigel"

"He's a bit shy!"

"He's very cute!"

"I found him on the street!
He was crying into a kebab
you should have seen the state he was in!
No idea what his real name is!
He had no identification on him and I've not been able to trace his owner,
so I thought I'd just call him Nigel!"
"He looks like a Nigel don't you think?"

"Yes! Definitely "a Nigel I'd say"

"Hello Nigel"

"You won't get much out of him I'm afraid!" He's a bit"

"Yes! Shy! You said!"

"Don't do that Nigel!
I keep telling him! It's not nice to stare but he seems to be infatuated by Breasts!"
"NIGEL!!"
"I am trying to train him! He's a rescue man you know!"

"Yes you said!" "Have you taken him to alcoholics anonymous? Someone there might know him!

"Noooo!
"I've not let him in the house yet!
He lives in the shed!
He seems happy in there!
You should see his little face when I let him go!!
Straight into the shed"
"Nigel!! Stop that!!

" He gets a little excited when he meets new people"

"Down Nigel!!

"No! No! put it away!!

"Look I'm going to have to go! Don't want him to shit in the road again!

"Goodbye Vicar!

"Good boy Nigel! Good boy!"
"Now let's get you home!"

Things I miss most

The things I miss most
is those heartfelt hello's
the nods and the winks and
the mind how you go's
that smile from a stranger
that glance too and fro
the all too familiar
from a face that you know

The things I miss most
are the friends past away
the things that you shared
and the things they would say
I miss the odd banter
the pint and the crack
the memories once shared
and the joy looking back

The things I miss most
are those fun-filled days
the innocent fun
in the sun drenched haze
the building of friendships
fighting through tears
the making of times
that would last through the years

The things I miss most
is the home made jam
when father was dad
and me mother was mam
when apples were scrumped
and lessons were taught
when God helped the children
if ever were caught

The things I miss most
is the every day
the old and familiar
the things people say
hello to the fairies
how do you do
Moghrey-mie to the morning
and a yesser to you

Ode to Illiam

with man and musket duly primed
lead-out the innocent and blind

and through the stillness of the day
I still hear the ricochet

Thanks for the memories

In the laze of the day
I while away memories
dusting off the old
with thoughts of putting them back into
Well!
some kind of order

The long lost and the forgotten
jump out and in
jostling, for positions not rightfully theirs
Bare bones long since buried
spring!
like Jacks from out their closets
hurriedly they deposit their soil
Spoils!
to end the recall of a perfect day
A deep breath
plus a sip of brew
puts them to rest
and so bereft
brings again sweet memories into view

First kiss
First love
First job
First child
First tooth
First shoes
First full night sleep
from weeks on weeks of night time blues
A first word!

(thanks for the memories cont:)

These firsts!
Have for me, repeated!
Repeatedly!
They punctuate my past
They sit
No!
They stand out!

They are the happiness
They are the happy in what life is all about
Well them and bikes
and the thousand other things I likes
the thousand beers I've drank
the thousand toasts I've raised and sank
the thousands that I've never made
nor ever made the banks
the thousand thing I've yet to do
before the few give thanks

On the sunny side of life

I'm still on the sunny side of the sod!
One of my favorite sayings!
Still dodging Gods
still undecided as to a final destination
I hesitate between the nothing
the hereafter and some eternal cremation
between sod, the sod-it or the sods damnation

Someone!
And it could easily have been me!
Said!
"There is only the now
and once you're gone you're…"
Not out loud,
Just loud enough to upset the believer in me!

Time will soon enough
degrade this soul
set free to ware
and whittle away the bones
where all but trace of my existence
there extinct

It is I think
in testament
to my promiscuity
I will exist only
in the spent dilute DNA
of some future celtish clone
till then I'm dodging Gods
I'm clinging to the sunnier side of sods

www.ingramcontent.com/pod-product-compliance
Lightning Source LLC
Chambersburg PA
CBHW020607220526
45463CB00006B/2482